A CHRISTIA
EMOTIONAL HEALING &
DELIVERANCE

Out of the
SNARE

GLENN DORSEY

Out of the Snare:
A Christian's Guide to Emotional Healing & Deliverance
By Glenn Dorsey
3rd Edition

www.glenndorsey.org
glenndorseymin@gmail.com

ISBN: 978-1508925484

TABLE OF CONTENTS

FOREWORD

The breakdown of the family, the absence of fathers, and the consequences of rapid change in our culture are bringing people with intense emotional pain into the church. Pastors often experience frustration as they counsel this influx of people with severe spiritual wounds. Praying a simple prayer at the end of a brief counseling session seems to bring little comfort to these individuals with serious, ongoing needs.

Counseling, prayer, and spiritual warfare have an important place in ministry. However, a person with intense emotional pain and spiritual wounds needs more. They must be confronted with Truth before healing can occur.

The Word of God is that confrontational Truth and can do what no person can. "For the word of God *is* living and powerful, and sharper than any two-edged sword, piercing even to the division of soul and spirit, and of joints and marrow, and is a discerner of the thoughts and intents of the heart" (Hebrews 4:12, NKJV).

An individual's actions are based on beliefs he assumes to be truth. Sadly, people with emotional trauma often have beliefs about themselves and their life situations that are not true. *False beliefs bring deception and bondage.*

My goal in this book is to present a scriptural method for healing emotional pain. Our provision for healing is centered in the crucifixion of Jesus Christ. Jesus said, "You will know the truth, and the truth will set you free" (John 8:32, ESV). We must know truth if we are to be free. Truth is the medicine of emotional healing. The pharmacy is the Bible, and the physician is the Holy Spirit.

It is also my prayer that this book gives understanding about the manifestation of certain spirits of oppression in human behavior and how these can be confronted.

May you be strengthened and empowered as you pursue emotional healing and deliverance through Jesus Christ!

—The Author

CHAPTER 1

LOOSE
THEM AND
LET THEM GO

This is not a ministry I asked for. In 1995, I was like most every other pastor. I cared for my people. I listened to their problems. I prayed over their needs. I sought the Lord for sermons that would instruct, direct, and encourage the believers in my flock.

And like most every other pastor, I had my share of counseling sessions. It wasn't uncommon for a person with deep emotional pain to stop by seeking help. In their distress, many shared their most personal secrets, looking to me for any answer or glimmer of hope I could offer.

Too often, I had nothing to give. I would reach into my most profound experiences—my limited assortment of life experiences and wisdom—and come up clutching lint. Peter once told a lame man, "Silver and gold I do not have, but what I do have I give you" (Acts 3:6, NKJV). In my case, I had more silver and gold than healing. Year after year, I sent hurting people away with only a promise. "I'll be praying for you," I would say. It seemed futile, insincere, and superficial.

That changed one Saturday night in my study. As I prayed, the Spirit of God moved me to put away the sermon I had prepared for the next morning. He directed me toward the story of Absalom, the handsome son of King David, who had been banished from the king's court for killing a stepbrother.

I peered deeply into the story. After he killed his brother, Absalom fled to another country and had no contact with is father. Joab, commander of Israel's army and advisor to the king, observed David's ongoing grief over the absence of his son. Joab enlisted a wise woman to approach David with a story.

According to 2 Samuel 14, the woman disguised herself and met the king as he passed along the road. She told him that her two sons had argued, and one had killed the other. Now, the family was demanding that the murderer be killed to avenge the loss of his brother. If such a thing happened, the woman cried, she would be bereft of both her sons.

David's compassion rose to defend this elderly mother. He gave his word as king that her living son, though a murderer, would not be harmed. She would not suffer the loss of two sons.

That's when the woman revealed her true purpose. She said, "Why then have you schemed such a thing against the people of God? For the king speaks this thing as one who is guilty, *in that* the king does not bring his banished one home again. For we will surely die and *become* like water spilled on the ground, which cannot be gathered up again. Yet God does not take away a life; but He devises means, so that His banished ones are not expelled from Him" (2 Samuel 14:13–14, NKJV).

The words struck me like a thunderbolt! They were an amazing revelation of the grace and mercy of God. We, too, have been outcast. We, too, have stood far from God, yet the Father has made a way for us to return home. The sacrificial death of Jesus Christ opened the gate home. The Father has not given up on us—He has devised a way to restore the relationship and fellowship He desires with each of us!

The next morning, I shared the message with the congregation. On Monday, a young man I'll call *Roy* came to my office weeping. His first words were, "Pastor, yesterday you saved my life! Your message saved my life!"

Roy told me that the night before he placed a loaded gun to his head in his automobile. He was about to pull the trigger when his wife walked into the garage and saw him. But her interruption only delayed what he was determined to do. His plan was to end his life after church Sunday afternoon.

That's where God stepped in! The Holy Spirit had given him hope. He realized his heavenly Father had devised a way for him to return home.

He went on to relate what made him suicidal. From age nine until he was a young teenager, a mentally handicapped uncle had sexually molested him. Repeated attacks had shattered his childhood and left open wounds in his soul. The shame, the lost innocence, and the guilt he lived with were more than he could handle, he explained.

With desperation in his eyes, this wounded soul pleaded with me to help him. It was a dilemma I faced many times in a quarter century of pastoring. It was obvious that this young man needed more than platitudes and shallow prayers. He looked to me with searching eyes, needing help that could only come from above.

What happened that wonderful Monday morning was the culmination of God's direct intervention in my life. It ushered me into a new and powerful phase of ministry. We prayed, and God stepped in! Roy was healed from the inside out. Joy and peace filled a heart once boiling over with guilt and shame.

Looking back, I realize that for quite some time the Holy Spirit had been setting me up for change.

A few years earlier, the Lord placed me in Burkina Faso, West Africa, where I met a pastor in the middle of a desert. His name was Pastor Bari. The natives called his church "the lunatic church".

What I saw shocked me! I was raised in church all my life. I heard about demoniacs, but had never seen one! There in the African desert, I saw demoniacs chained to tree stumps and locked in clay houses, moving constantly, screaming, and writhing. People who were critically ill and dying laid in the shade of small buildings. It so happed that a film crew from Assemblies of God World Missions was visiting Pastor Bari during my stay.

During a filmed interview, the pastor told the following story. After his conversion as a young man, the Lord burned Matthew 18:19 into his heart: "Again I say to you that if two of you agree on earth concerning anything that they ask, it will be done for them by My Father in heaven" (NKJV). Using that promise, Pastor Bari and his wife began praying for the sick and demon-possessed people in his area. God powerfully set them free! Word spread. Many afflicted people began showing up at their doorstep, seeking his help. Twice a day he and his wife would pray for them. They would step outside their home and begin to laugh, praising God for what He was going to do! Then the husband and wife would proceed toward whomever had arrived for help. The demon possessed individuals would fall on the ground as the couple approached. They would lay hands on the tormented individuals and pray in faith.

I was fascinated! Pastor Bari's entire congregation consisted of those who had been healed and delivered. As we prepared to leave, I could not resist asking Pastor Bari to pray for me.

Shall I say, "I made a major mistake?" Only God knows! I asked him to pray that God would give me a *little* of what he had. If I could relive that moment, I would ask for so much more!

Humble Pastor Bari laid his hands on me and prayed for God to use me. I had no way of knowing what God had planned for my future.

Sometime later, I was dramatically affected by the Brownsville Revival. Brownsville Assembly of God in Pensacola, Florida, experienced a wonderful moving of God's Spirit. Thousands were saved. I visited and witnessed first-hand the power of God.

During a trip to the revival, I heard about a woman named Theresa Castleman. Theresa ministered deliverance for those with special needs attending the services. God used her to open my eyes to spiritual warfare. I would never have been open to her teaching had it not been for West Africa.

A CHURCH FILLED WITH VICTIMS

Just before Easter, I took 120 people from our church to Pensacola. Something amazing happened to us! What began as a traditional revival service, extended into six weeks of revival. One night during the revival services, the Holy Spirit asked me a most unusual question.

"What do your closest friends have in common?"

I was startled by my answer—child abuse! A host of people in the audience had been victimized or affected by child abuse. The Holy Spirit let me scan the crowd and see them as I had never seen them before. He whispered, "Your church is full of victims of child abuse. I want you to preach on the life of Mephibosheth, and call your sermon "The Victim."

Mephibosheth was the son of Jonathan, King David's closest friend until slain in battle. As a child, Mephibosheth was forced to flee from advancing Philistines. In the haste, the young boy was dropped by a servant responsible for caring for him. His feet were mangled so badly in the fall, he never recovered. Mephibosheth was crippled the rest of his life. For many years, he was also an outcast. King David sought him out, loved him for Jonathan's sake, and restored Jonathan's estate and possessions to him.

What a picture of so many lives today! Many people are like Mephibosheth—spiritual cripples, victimized through no fault of their own, living as outcasts and fugitives from God. Like Mephibosheth, their injuries were not caused by anything they had done, but because of neglect or sinfulness by authority figures in their lives. These wounds never heal until Jesus is sought out and showers them with mercy and grace, and restores their rightful possessions to them.

I had never seen it so clearly before.

What followed, changed the entire course of our church and my ministry. God began equipping us to help hurting people. He was making our church slogan reality: "A place for the hurt to heal and a new life to begin." We knew we had been enlisted for a warfare that was new to us.

We can only minister the truth we know.

It came full circle when I sat face-to-face with young Roy that breakthrough Monday morning in my office. Realizing his need and the work God was asking me to do, with His help, sent me urgently seeking an understanding of God's Word and the spirit world.

God brought other means of instruction into my path. My brother attended a church in Oklahoma that had begun a ministry for people with emotional pain. And with the help of another pastor, I saw a powerful, life-changing transformation in Roy. The anger he had carried most of his life was broken; he was free of it! Other issues in his life would be confronted later by our own church ministry team, leading Roy to give a very moving and public testimony of the new freedom in his life.

Each of these events tugged and pushed me toward a ministry for people needing emotional healing or deliverance. It was not a ministry I chose for myself. God chose it for me, and He chooses best. And because it is His work, He provides all I lack. Now, when I am confronted by a distraught, tormented soul, I know what the Master wishes to do. I am aware of His presence and His power. I realize He knows His foe, and has compassion on His wounded child. I sense His presence with me, supplying the discernment, authority and power necessary to destroy the work of Satan.

I watch God work through His Word and Spirit, and I rejoice.

Emotional healing and deliverance are topics that spark debate among many Christians. The tendency is to lump all such ministries together and judge them from the perspective of our limited, personal experience. Most ministers acknowledge the tragedy caused by spiritual bondage, destructive habits, and deception. Many can recognize the symptoms, but few understand the cause, and fewer still commit themselves to the battle of setting victims free.

Jesus said, "You shall know the truth, and the truth shall make you free" (John 8:32, NKJV). If we do not hear truth, we cannot embrace it. If it is not embraced, it will do us no good. So, then, it is the truth we know and embrace that makes us free!

Once the Lord opened my heart to help people with emotional wounds and spiritual bondage, He began bringing them to our church from all walks of life. This is the wisdom of God—the Father will not send His children to people who cannot minister to their needs. This helped us realize our responsibility to prepare to serve greater numbers.

A church must prepare for this type of ministry. Only the truth we know can make us free. Likewise, *we can only minister the truth we know.* While a lack of knowledge and understanding causes fear and division. Beginning with our leaders, we began building a team of respected believers who were accountable, trustworthy, confidential in their dealing, and known for their intercessory prayer. We trained in the Word and prayed in the Spirit for wisdom, discernment, power, and guidance.

We didn't have long to wait. God sent hurting people from all walks of life—from every imaginable ethnic group, culture, and social status. He sent pastors and believers from numerous denominations. They came as teachers, missionaries, evangelists, deacons, licensed professional counselors, businessmen, housewives, students, blue collar workers, roughneck, and the like. They came with every conceivable problem. We met them at the altar and in the prayer room, and, like Peter and John, we gave them what we had.

Carlos Anacondia is an internationally known evangelist from Argentina who has conducted revival crusades for multitudes throughout Central and South America. He has a trained team of individuals who ministers to those needing deliverance. Those who are "demonized" or "possessed" are taken by the hundreds to tents behind the open-air stadiums where he preaches. There, God delivers the oppressed, possessed, and heals the sick, just as He did in New Testament times.

Evangelist Anacondia said that 60% of these converts go on to become active in the local church. He also said, "You cannot have revival without deliverance being a part of it."

I believe every church proclaiming Jesus is the Christ should have such a ministry available to believers. Any church reaching the lost will bring into its midst people with personal histories of abuse and bondage, who do not know how to conduct themselves in the Lord's house. Jesus has given them a new spirit and made them a new creation, yet they struggle with a carnal past and an old way of thinking. They need emotional healing. They need deliverance.

They are conceptually similar to Lazarus, who was raised to new life, but bound in grave clothes.

"Jesus said to them, 'Loose him, and let him go.'" (John 11:44, NKJV).

Jesus still calls out to those dead in trespasses and sin. He still gives life to people with no hope. He still penetrates hearts with light, dispels deception, and infuses with truth from above.

He brings to us those now alive in Christ, but bound with past hurts, destructive habits, or wrong beliefs. These bindings wrap God's children to their past like grave clothes. They squeeze out victory and joy, and they seek to drag them back into the pit.

With tender instruction, unconditional love, ever-enduring patience, and gentle maturity, we must help them learn to walk in the law of liberty in Christ Jesus.

We must do the work of God. We must loose them and let them go.

CHAPTER ONE
DISCUSSION QUESTIONS

1. Have you ever had someone share private pain with you and you didn't know what to do or say? How did you go about helping them?

2. What has God done for us to make a way for us to return to him? Read 2 Samuel 14:14. Discuss.

3. According to John 8:32, what makes us free?

4. According to John 11:44 what is the assignment of the church to oppressed and victimized people? Discuss.

CHAPTER 2

THE CROSS IS ENOUGH

T his ministry of "loosing" souls is not new. It isn't an old doctrine made contemporary with a new term. The sacred mission of the church has always been to bring God's redeemed into the full measure of liberty and freedom in Christ.

Many have been saved. Each one is, indeed, a new creation in Christ (2 Corinthians 5:17). God has breathed into each His divine Spirit, adopting them totally and completely as His own dear children.

The Spirit of God then goes to work. The Holy Spirit begins to rearrange priorities, purify desires, and re-shape character. His goal is to mold the believer into the very image of Christ (Romans 8:29).

Our sanctification is neither an overnight, one-step process, nor painless. The Bible describes it as a war within our members (Romans 7:23). The Spirit begins to take charge—to call into account—the old desires of our sinful nature. Step by step, God's Spirit leads us into alignment with His will. Though we are forgiven of iniquity, He begins working to impress His image onto us. He calls forward wrong habits, unforgiveness, bitterness, and undisciplined areas in our lives. Patiently, He gives us the opportunity to renounce each shortcoming, to turn from the old way, and begin living under the reign of His spirit. Sometimes old desires die hard, and here the Master proves the sufficiency of His grace. Sometimes we refuse to budge, even after His tender but insistent prodding. Here we camp, unable to move forward in our spiritual growth or closer in fellowship with our dear Redeemer, until the desire for Him proves stronger than our desire for fleshly things. We repent, He washes us in the fountains of forgiveness, and our journey toward sanctification begins once again.

And yet, sometimes we find an area in our spiritual and emotional composition that simply does not conform to the call of the Spirit, no matter how much we seem to desire it to change. I have known individuals who have cried out to God night and day to be free of unreasonable fear, destructive and violent outbursts, or the lure sexual sin. The failure to be free, even after much anguish and tears, leaves them with feelings of guilt, defeat, and even despair.

What causes these areas of bondage in a life? Why do some individuals seem unable to slip free from them as easily as forgiveness was found on the day of salvation?

To answer these questions, consider Jesus' provision through His suffering and death on the cross as it relates to the entire man—body, soul, and spirit.

"But he was pierced for our transgressions; he was crushed for our iniquities; upon him was the chastisement that brought us peace, and with his wounds we are healed. All we like sheep have gone astray; we have turned—every one—to his own way; and the Lord has laid on him the iniquity of us all. (Isaiah 53:5–6, ESV).

We know with great confidence that Jesus died for our sins. We know with great confidence that He died for our healing. Knowing this to be truth, do we still sin? Do we continue to become sick? The answer, of course, is **yes**.

What do we do when we sin? What do we do when we are sick? We return to the place of power: the cross! 1 Peter 2:24 says Jesus "bore our sins in His own body on the tree, that we, having died to sins, might live for righteousness—by whose stripes you were healed" (NKJV). So, then, the blood of Jesus continues to cleanse us of sin, and His stripes continue to heal our sicknesses.

The victory of the cross is final, finished, and forever. The provision of the cross never ends! The cross is the place for salvation. The cross is the place for healing. The cross has power over all the effects of sin!

Isaiah's beautiful passage about the Messiah contained this description of His suffering: "He was oppressed and He was afflicted, yet He opened not His mouth" (Isaiah 53:7, NKJV).

JESUS WAS OPPRESSED

Jesus himself was oppressed of the devil.

Jesus was oppressed! Indeed, He is Immanuel, God with us. He has in every way been tested as a man, yet He did not sin. He understands torment and vexation of the human soul, and knows well the source of all temptation. He was oppressed in the Garden of Gethsemane. Because He was, "We do not have a High Priest who cannot sympathize with our weaknesses, but was in all points tempted as we are, yet without sin" (Hebrews 4:15, NKJV).

Our Lord identified Himself with us! "He took with Him Peter and the two sons of Zebedee, and He began to be sorrowful and deeply distressed. Then He said to them, 'My soul is exceedingly sorrowful, even to death.'" (Matthew 26:37–38, NKJV).

A little later, "being in an agony he prayed more earnestly: and his sweat was as it were great drops of blood falling down to the ground" (Luke 22:44, KJV).

This was the One Isaiah called "despised and rejected by men, a Man of sorrows and acquainted with grief" (Isaiah 53:3, NKJV).

Jesus Himself was oppressed of the devil. He understood and helped others overcome oppression! Peter testified "how God anointed Jesus of Nazareth with the Holy Spirit and with power, who went about doing good and healing all who were oppressed by the devil, for God was with Him" (Acts 10:38, NKJV). Luke the physician recorded those words of Peter, and verified that oppression can be healed.

Are you oppressed? Are you in trouble? Do you need a refuge? "The LORD also will be a refuge for the oppressed, a refuge in times of trouble" (Psalm 9:8,NKJV).

TWO TYPES OF SICKNESS

Matthew 4:24 gives two types of sickness. "They brought to Him all sick people who were afflicted

23

with various disease and torments . . . and He healed them" (NKJV)

The term used for torment is the Greek word *basanos*. Three times the New Testament uses this word, which Strong's Concordance defines as torture, acute pains, and the pains of a disease, even the agony of those in hell after death. It implies the notion of "going to the bottom."

Perhaps you feel you have gone to the bottom and cannot lift yourself. Thank the Lord that Jesus is our healer! He is the lifter of our head (Psalm 3:3). We are always within His reach.

"And it shall come to pass that whoever calls on the name of the LORD shall be saved" (Joel 2:32, NKJV).

Peter knew how to call out to God in distress. "But the boat was now in the middle of the sea, tossed with waves, for the wind was contrary. Now in the fourth watch of the night, Jesus went to them, walking on the sea. And when the disciples saw Him walking on the sea, they were troubled, saying 'It is a ghost!' and they cried out for fear. But immediately Jesus spoke to them, saying, 'Be of good cheer! It is I; do not be afraid.' And Peter answered Him and said, 'Lord, if it is You, command me come to You on the water.' So He said, 'Come.' And when Peter had come down out of the boat, he walked on the water to go to Jesus. But when he saw that the wind was boisterous, he was afraid; and beginning to sink he cried, saying, 'Lord, save me!' And immediately Jesus stretched out His hand and caught him, 'O you of little faith, why did you doubt?'" (Matthew 14:24–31, NKJV).

It may seem that your night will never end. You may have contrary winds of oppression disturbing your life. It is then that Jesus comes to His disciples, walking on the sea.

Jesus taught us marvelous truths in this story. First, contrary winds were hindering progress and threatening the ship with overwhelming waves. The sea was the problem, and Jesus walked on the problem toward His disciples.

Peter knew the safest place in a storm was there beside Jesus.

Jesus invited Peter to come to Him. While others feared, Peter took a great step of faith. Like his Master, he too, walked on water. Peter walked on his problems!

All was well until Peter took his gaze off of Jesus. He began to focus on the power of the wind or storm. Immediately he started to sink.

Such may be true with you. You may have full confidence in who Jesus is. You probably remember times He visited you in a storm. You may have even walked by faith at one time, but somehow, life can cause focus to shift. Maybe you no longer see the Savior's face just ahead. You may only see the storm. The incessant wind brings a feeling of being battered and oppressed. You could be living in the middle of the devastation it caused.

We can magnify oppression until we lose faith, or we can call out on the One who stands tall above our problem. Jesus is *not* sinking. He can command any oppressive spirit to stop harassing you.

The response of Jesus is always the same. When we cry aloud, His response is immediate. "Immediately Jesus stretched out His hand and caught him." The strong grip of the Lord caught him and delivered him from his distress.

When I was a child, my father often took me fishing. A particular place he enjoyed most was a river where the current was swift and no deeper than my waist. My father decided he wanted to cross the river and fish from the other side. Taking tackle in one hand and my hand in the other, we started across. The rocks were slippery and made standing difficult for a child. But what seemed like deep water to me was nothing to my father.

During one trek across the strong current, my feet were swept suddenly from the rocks. Water rushed over me! Fear overwhelmed me! I sensed I was headed downstream to die. Then, just as suddenly as I was launched into the rapid flow, I stopped. My dad held my hand with a grip so firm and sure I knew it would not turn loose. Father caught me and eased my fear with words that all was well. We would make it to the other side.

We have a heavenly Father who will not let us be swept away as long as we trust in Him. "Yes, He loves the people; all His saints are in Your hand" (Deuteronomy 33:3, NKJV).

"What then shall we say to these things? If God *is* for us, who can be against us? He who did not spare His own Son, but delivered Him up for us all, how shall He not with Him also freely give us all things? Who shall bring a charge against God's elect? *It is* God who justifies. Who *is* he who condemns? It *is* Christ who died, and furthermore is also risen, who is even at the right hand of God, who also makes intercession for us. Who shall separate us from the love of Christ? *Shall* tribulation, or distress, or persecution, or famine, or nakedness, or peril, or sword? For I am persuaded that neither death nor life, nor angels nor principalities nor powers, nor things present nor things to come, nor height nor depth, nor any other created thing, shall be able to separate us from the love of God which is in Christ Jesus our Lord" (Romans 8:31–36,38–39, NKJV).

"I give them eternal life, and they shall never perish; neither shall anyone snatch them out of My hand" (John 10:28, NKJV).

You will cross to the other side! The grip of our Father will save you.

The message of Jesus has never changed. He was sent to heal the brokenhearted, proclaim liberty to the captive, and open the prison to those who are bound (Isaiah 61:1). His Spirit is still working today with the power to bind, loose, set free, and comfort.

He is not the Jesus who *was*. He is the Jesus who *is*. He "*is* the same yesterday, today, and forever" (Hebrews 13:8, NKJV), and He desires to work powerfully in your life today.

> *You will cross to the other side! The grip of our Father will save you.*

Before Jesus died, He cried, "It is finished!" The Greek word used for "finished" is *tetelestai*, which means paid in full. Jesus paid the full price for the whole man—spirit, soul, and body. He brings eternal life to the spirit, healing to the body, and renewal to the mind.

Consequently, any principality or power that comes against a believer has been disarmed by the cross. Paul wrote: "And you, being dead in your trespasses and the uncircumcision of your flesh, He has made alive together with Him, having forgiven you all trespasses, having wiped out the handwriting of requirements that was against us, which was contrary to us. And He has taken it out of the way, having nailed it to the cross. Having disarmed principalities and powers, He made a public spectacle of them, triumphing over them in it" (Colossians 2:13–15, NKJV).

The crown of thorns thrust on the head of Jesus was symbolic of the curse placed upon man in the Garden. Christ became a curse for us.

"Christ has redeemed us from the curse of the law, having become a curse for us (for it is written, 'Cursed is everyone who hangs on a tree'), that the blessing of Abraham might come upon the Gentiles in Christ Jesus, that we might receive the promise of the Spirit through faith" (Galatians 3:13–14, NKJV).

Because he has redeemed us from the curse by becoming a curse for us, by faith we can break the pattern of sin and sickness.

Often I am asked, "If we are a new creature in Christ, and all things have become new, and if we are genuinely saved, why does a person need emotional healing?"

My answer is simply this: At the moment of salvation we receive eternal life, a renewed mind, and the promise of an incorruptible body. We are given a future in which our steps are ordered of the Lord. The Holy Spirit begins guiding us into all

29

truth. Yet our minds contain a composite of life's events that must be filtered through the Spirit and healed. The Holy Spirit works in our present, while God is planning our future.

One major weapon Satan uses against us is the past. We cannot erase our memories. It is not uncommon for traumatic events to be buried in the subconscious. We say to ourselves, *I just want to forget that horrible incident and get on with my life.*

But an issue not healed will eventually resurface. An event may have been so traumatic that it is blocked out for years, but suddenly without warning, flashbacks can occur. Emotional scars may begin showing themselves as unreasonable reactions to common-place events of life.

A Christian may need emotional healing because the pain of the past prevents him from receiving God's best in the present. Barriers exist that he cannot get past; these affect his relationship with God. When he seeks God, he seems to run into a wall.

Our self-esteem, how we relate to others, and how we make decisions are all based upon past events in our lives.

Once I asked a person to stop praying "God" and begin praying "Father." She replied with a shocking question, "Do I have to call Him Father?

My father molested me. I don't like calling Him Father."

Was she saved? Yes. Was she heaven-bound? Yes. Was she free from emotional wounds? No. John 8:32 says, "You shall know the truth and the truth shall make you free" (NKJV).

So the process of emotional healing, often a very necessary part of our sanctification, takes us back to the cross to confront the past and receive the healing Jesus purchased for us through the stripes on His back. Just as He heals the body, so He heals the emotions. In so doing, He restores the soul.

The cross of Christ Jesus has provided healing for the entire person.

CHAPTER TWO
DISCUSSION QUESTIONS

1. How and when was Jesus oppressed?

2. According to Matthew 4:24 there are two types of sickness. What are they? How are they different? Explain.

3. According to Colossians 2:13–15, what did Jesus do with our enemies at the cross?

4. How does one's past affect his or her:

> A. relationship with God the Father?
> B. future?
> C. self-esteem?

5. At what three levels of your person does the cross bring victory to your life? Explain.

CHAPTER 3

OPPRESSION EXPLAINED

I saiah wrote of Jesus: "He was oppressed" (Isaiah 53:7, NKJV). If the Son of God could be oppressed of the devil, shouldn't we expect similar harassment?

The word "oppress" comes from the Hebrew word *nagas,* which Strong's Concordance translates "to harass, distress, to drive an animal, a workman or a debtor." In the Greek, the same word is *katadunasteuo,* which means "to exercise dominion against."

Here lies the key to understanding the source of many emotional dysfunctions. "For we do not wrestle against flesh and blood, but against principalities, against powers, against the rulers of the darkness of this age, against spiritual *hosts* of wickedness in heavenly *places*" (Ephesians 6:12, NKJV).

Could it be that a dramatic mood shift might be caused by a spirit? Is it conceivable that a sudden outburst of anger might be provoked by an opponent in the unseen realm? Should we believe that irrational fears, panic attacks, and phobias which leave us isolated from the world and unable to function, may well be the signature work of dark forces that exist to enslave us and undermine the purpose of God for our lives?

The Bible tells us clearly this is so! Satan and his demonic host are organized to bring oppression against every believer!

Not long ago, the Discovery Channel aired a program about lionesses. I was quite absorbed with the sight of a pride of lions attacking a herd of water buffalo. The water buffalo is said to be among the strongest animals in the wild. Imagine the strength in a herd of hundreds! Yet, a small group of eight or nine lionesses skillfully maneuvered themselves until they isolated one buffalo from the herd and encircled it.

I was amazed how they brought down the buffalo. A lioness grabbed each leg of the animal and held on. Another gripped the buffalo's neck and literally hung upside down. None bit the buffalo; they just attached themselves and refused to let go. The rest of the pride jumped onto the buffalo's back.

All the while the buffalo struggled. He tried to gore the lions with his horns. He could not kick. He could not run. He could merely sling his head and stand. After a short time, even standing became an exerted effort. The buffalo began to stagger from the collective weight. One lioness then ran underneath the standing buffalo and ripped open its stomach. The buffalo fell, prey to the group.

The Holy Spirit spoke to me and said, "See how a person is taken by oppression? It is not one issue in a person's life, but rather a continual attack of issues that won't go away. A person becomes isolated from a group of believers and is overcome with life."

"Be sober, be vigilant; because your adversary the devil walks about like a roaring lion, seeking whom he may devour" (1 Peter 5:8, NKJV).

Jesus said, "The thief does not come except to steal, and to kill, and to destroy. I have come that they may have life, and that they may have *it* more abundantly" (John 10:10, NKJV).

How do we know the enemy is present in our life? Consider that our unseen enemy is much like a gentle breeze. Can you see the wind? No. How do you know it is there? You can feel it. You can see some movement as it passes. A blade of grass trembles, a branch sways, or a leaf is torn loose and falls to the ground. From the evidence, we know a breeze is present. We can determine the direction from which it comes and the force of its strength. If we see trees falling we know it is a strong wind.

It is the same in the spirit world. Often we can sense the presence of darkness. Other times, we have only to look at the turmoil, confusion, envy, or hurt left in its wake to realize its presence.

When we are victimized repeatedly by a particular type of sin or harmful habit—such as lying or gossiping—and cannot maintain victory over it, we can conclude an oppressive spirit has come against us, found a legitimate right to harass us, and has set up camp. This is a strong man, and his meddling in our affairs is a stronghold. Only when the strongman is discovered and his strategy against us revealed can
we bind this oppressing spirit and be free of its influence.

WHAT IS OPPRESSION?

Oppression is manipulation of the body by a spirit. Possession occurs when a spirit gains control of the body. Oppression is an attack on the mind. Possession is achieved when a spirit has captured the mind. Oppression is an assault by a spirit outside the body. Possession means a spirit dwells within the human body. Oppression is caused when a person lives on a carnal, self-indulgent, or sensory plane. Possession allows a spirit to abuse the body.

The Scriptures clearly teach that a Christian cannot be possessed by a demonic spirit. God and

Satan cannot inhabit the same dwelling. However, a Christian may be "oppressed" or tormented re-repeatedly by a spirit through a stronghold of the mind. Often, because of past sin or an unintended wound to the spirit, an evil spirit has legal right to afflict a person—even a Christian—while not totally controlling or possessing the individual.

Oppression is an attack on the mind.

Pastors often call and describe a believer who has manifested strange physical reactions during an anointed church service. They ask, "Is that person possessed?"

The answer is, no. A believer cannot belong to God and be possessed against his will by a demonic spirit. Still, where there is great anointing of the Holy Spirit, physical manifestations occur which appear to be demonic but are not.

To understand this more fully requires knowing a person's relationship (or lack of one) with the Lord. It also requires that we be able to discern the spirit to know what kind of spirit is harassing the believer.

The Word of God has the ability to discern the spirit of a man. "For the word of God is living and powerful, and sharper than any two-edged sword, piercing even to the division of soul and spirit, and of joints and marrow, and is a discerner of the thoughts and intents of the heart" (Hebrews 4:12, NKJV).

Luke 8:26–38 gives us an account showing some characteristics of a demon-possessed individual:

- Living in harsh conditions or unconventional environments *(he lived in the tombs, v. 27)*

- Nakedness *(v. 27)*

- Loud voice *(v. 28)*

- Compulsive, driven or out of control behavior *(he was driven by the demon into the wilderness, v. 29)*

- A change of voice *(demons spoke to Jesus from this man, v. 30)*

- Supernatural strength *(chains could not hold him, v. 29)*

- Insanity *(when he was delivered, he was in his right mind, v. 35)*

- Cutting the body or self-destructiveness *(he cut himself with stones Mark 5:5)*

While taking someone I'll call *Rudy* through the emotional healing process, we began to deal with his main issue, anger. He came from a family with a reputation for anger. Rudy recounted stories about angry outbursts by family members going back three generations. After teaching him what the Bible says about anger, I laid my hands on Rudy and began to rebuke a spirit of anger. During my prayer, the young man fell out of his chair and onto the floor. His tongue thickened and his language became slurred. He attempted to speak, but could not.

I knew this man quite well. He loved and served God. He had been faithful as a father and husband. There was absolutely no doubt in my mind of his relationship with the Lord. Yet there he was, lying on the floor in front of me, unable to speak clearly.

I realized the spirit of anger was losing its hold on Rudy. I instructed him to begin to speak the name of Jesus. He began to attempt to say the name; with each utterance, his speech became clearer. After a short time, it became normal.

Rudy began to grin. He got up from the floor, and with boldness and authority, he rebuked the spirit of anger that had dominated his life. He knew the stronghold had fallen, and he rejoiced! What a wonderful victory we observed that day!

Rudy had not been *possessed*, but *oppressed* by a spirit of anger. God had set him free! When the truth of God's Word is being preached or taught with anointing, truth is received and applied. If an oppressing spirit is present, it may manifest itself in one form or another. If we take authority over the spirit in the name of Jesus, there will be a reaction.

A pastor asked me to minister to a woman who had been severely traumatized as a child. The woman, who had been saved only recently, was trapped in an abusive marriage. My pastor friend felt she was in desperate need of emotional healing.

The woman came promptly at the scheduled time. She appeared to be a lady in her fifties. Her hair was disheveled; her clothes were crumpled, and she walked stooped over. It was quite apparent she had no self-esteem.

As she entered the room, her voice changed to that of a whining little girl. Immediately I told her to stand up straight, take control of her body, and stop yielding it to a spirit of oppression. Almost instantly her normal voice returned, and I began the ministry session. The Lord performed a tremendous healing in her life. The Lord so drastically changed her that when she entered the Sunday worship service the following week, no one, including the pastor, recognized her.

WHERE OPPRESSION ATTACKS

The Apostle Paul gave us insight into the oppressing attacks of Satan. "For though we walk in the flesh, we do not war according to the flesh. For the weapons of our warfare are not carnal but mighty in God for pulling down strongholds, casting down arguments and every high thing that exalts itself against the knowledge of God, bringing every thought into captivity to the obedience of Christ" (2 Corinthians 10: 3–5, NKJV).

From these verses we understand that a stronghold is a thought that does not line up or agree with the truth of God's word. In other words, a stronghold begins with deception, and deception occurs when we believe something to be true that is not. When we believe in error, we allow ourselves to be trapped and held captive by wrong belief that cannot ascend to God's perfect plan and will.

God made man in three components: spirit, soul, and body.

The spirit of man is God-conscious. It is that integral part of every individual that yearns for our Father God. Jesus said, "No one can enter the kingdom of God unless he is born of water and the Spirit. Flesh gives birth to flesh, but the Spirit gives birth to spirit. You should not be surprised at My saying, 'You must be born again'" (John 3:5–7, NIV).

For ye have not received the spirit of bondage again to fear; but ye have received the Spirit of adoption, whereby we cry, Abba, Father. The Spirit itself beareth witness with our spirit, that we are the children of God: And if children, then heirs; heirs of God, and joint-heirs with Christ; if so be that we suffer with *him*, that we may be also glorified together" (Romans 8: 15–17, KJV).

The body is appointed for death. When the body is resurrected, then our salvation will be complete. "Not only that, but we also who have the firstfruits of the Spirit, even we ourselves groan within ourselves, eagerly waiting for the adoption, the redemption of our body" (Romans 8:23, NKJV).

The soul is the "inward man." It consists of our mind, will, senses, and emotions. The mind must be renewed. "And do not be conformed to this world, but be transformed by the renewing of your mind, that you may prove what *is* that good and acceptable and perfect will of God" (Romans 12:2, NKJV).

The mind is renewed only by dwelling or meditating on truth. 2 Timothy 1:7 says God has given us a sound mind. Living our life based on the reasoning of the carnal mind will always lead to oppression.

DOORS OF OPPORTUNITY

The spirit of oppression attacks the mind. Generally speaking, there are four "doors" of opportunity that allow oppressing spirits to enter our lives.

First, they enter through generational curses or sins. God said He would visit "the iniquity of the fathers upon the children to the third and fourth generations" (Exodus 20:5, NKJV). A family history of poverty, specific illness, premature death, physical abuse, adultery, divorce, anger, illegitimacy, racial prejudice, child abandonment, addictions, pride and the like are patterns of curses or sins passed down the family tree. Generational sins and tendencies can be passed down from father to child or from mother to child in much the same way a tendency to cancer or obesity can be bequeathed.

Oppressing spirits find opportunities through our bad decisions to torment us with guilt. The real issue here is self-forgiveness.

A young teenage driver returned home after a party in which he had a few drinks. A child riding a bicycle crossed the street and was struck and killed by the drunk driver. Years later the driver gave his life to Christ. Although he knew he had been forgiven for his deed, each time he saw a youngster on a bicycle, the young man was overcome with guilt. He could not shake free from remorse or the memory. His memory gave power to the past, and made yesterday seem as real as today.

Oppressing spirits also find opportunities through trauma, when an individual becomes a victim of circum-stances beyond his or her control.

A nine-year-old girl was sexually molested by a brother-in-law. Immediately a spirit of oppression began placing thoughts in her mind she perceived to be truth, but were not. Demonic spirits told her she deserved to be sexually exploited, that her body was the only thing of value she had to give others. The devil, who comes to steal, kill and destroy, stole her innocence and chained her in lies.

Satan is a master of deception. He works in the mind to implant lies, which shape the way we respond, view ourselves and others, and relate to God.

Sexual victims, for example, will usually have distorted beliefs of themselves, such as:

- "I wanted the abuse, therefore I am bad."

- "If I tell what happened, it will destroy my family, and I will be blamed."

- "I deserved what happened to me."

- "I deserve to be punished."

- "Love is supposed to hurt. Sex and love are the same."

- "I have no control or power over anything that happens to me."

- "No one will believe me or help me."

Are any of these thoughts true? Absolutely not! But by believing them, a stronghold is built in the mind by a lying spirit of oppression. A victim builds a belief system around himself. Like walls, these false notions provide a place of safety and protection to keep him from being hurt again. They are walls of false security. In reality, these walls create a place of loneliness, insecurity, and fear. It is a self-made prison. The walls that keep a person from being free to be himself must come down.

One may never erase the memories of the past, but thank the Lord, we can be healed of the emotional pain by the blessed power of the Word of God! Sound impossible? The healing Jesus brings is complete. The Word of God is not limited!

Finally, oppression can come to us through a satanic attack, which God permits.

Matthew 4 shows us how an attack of Satan can occur. After His flesh was weakened by a forty-day fast, the Son of God was attacked by Satan who questioned His identity.

Satan suggested that Jesus turn stones into bread. If Jesus had performed such a miracle, Satan would have succeeded in leading Jesus against the will of God. It was the will of God that Jesus fast and not eat. Furthermore, if Jesus had complied, He would have acted in His sovereign power as Son of God, and could never more be proclaimed as our great example. As Son of Man, it was necessary for Him to wait upon God for the answer to His need.

Satan suggested that Jesus leap from the highest point of the temple. He insinuated that if Jesus was the Son of God, no harm could come to Him. But had Jesus jumped, He would have violated the will of God. It was the Father's will that Jesus give His life on the cross, not prove His true identity through sensational theatrics that would require God's intervention if the divine plan were to be preserved.

Satan offered Jesus the world in exchange for His worship. This, too, would have thwarted the plan of God for Jesus' life. God's will was that Jesus go to the cross. If Jesus had taken Satan's offer and accepted the kingdoms of this world, there would have been no perfect, flawless Lamb sacrificed on the cross of Calvary. And because God had no "back-up plan," all hope for our salvation would have ended.

Satan often attacks after a time of physical exhaustion. He also often attacks before we embark upon the will of God for our life. Jesus came under attack before He performed His first public miracle. He was attacked before He preached His first sermon. He was attacked before He called His disciples.

PUT THE PAST BEHIND YOU

The second Adam, Jesus, was attacked much in the same way as the first Adam. Satan challenged them both using the Word of God. The first Adam succumbed and fell prey; the second Adam prevailed by knowing the Word and will of His Father.

Joseph, the youngest and most favored son of Jacob, had dreams of greatness. He told his family his dreams, and made his brothers envious. The years that followed were filled with pain, isolation, and despair. In prison, Joseph fought his memories. He fought bitterness and loneliness. Even so, the Lord was with Joseph, showing him mercy and favor. In time, God brought the fulfillment of His plans for Joseph's life. He was released from prison and promoted to second in power over all Egypt.

In the fruitful years that followed the trial, Joseph married and had two sons. The names of these sons indicated how he had struggled to overcome the hurts of his past. The eldest boy was named Manasseh, which means "causing to forget." The second son was named Ephraim, or "fruitfulness." Joseph had put the past behind him.

Then, one day, the very men who caused him such great harm stood before him needing food. All the memories and emotions of the past began to resurface. How would he deal with his offenders? He had the power to put them in prison or to death.

"Then Joseph could not restrain himself before all those who stood by him, and he cried out, 'Make everyone go out from me!' So no one stood with him while Joseph made himself known to his brothers. And he wept aloud, and the Egyptians and the house of Pharaoh heard it.

"Then Joseph said to his brothers, 'I *am* Joseph; does my father still live?' But his brothers could not answer him, for they were dismayed in his presence. And Joseph said to his brothers, 'Please come near to me.' So they came near. Then he said: 'I *am* Joseph your brother, whom you sold into Egypt. But now, do not therefore be grieved or angry with yourselves because you sold me here; for God sent me before you to preserve life. For these two years the famine *has been* in the land, and *there are* still five years in which *there will be* neither plowing nor harvesting. And God sent me before you to preserve a posterity for you in the earth, and to save your lives by a great deliverance. So now *it* was not you *who* sent me here, but God; and He has made me a father to Pharaoh, and lord of all his house, and a ruler throughout all the land of Egypt'" (Genesis 45:1–8, NKJV).

In those years of hardship and suffering, God had been working in the life of a man who would be used to preserve Israel in time of famine. Truly, painful memories can be healed! *We can have memories without pain.*

And we can apply the power of God's Word against every oppressing spirit. We can cast down every stronghold. We can take captive every thought that exalts itself against the knowledge of Christ. As we dispel deception and daily battle erroneous thoughts in our mind, we free ourselves from the web of lies and darkness that binds us. We grow steadily in truth, enlightenment, power and freedom.

Oppressing spirits can distress us, but through the power of the Word, we can gain the inevitable and ultimate victory!

Painful memories can be healed! We can have memories without pain.

CHAPTER THREE
DISCUSSION QUESTIONS

1. When people isolate themselves from others, what are some dangers that can occur to them spiritually?

2. What is oppression?

3. Make a list of some manifestations of oppression?

4. What is the difference between oppression and possession?

5. Explain what a stronghold is according to 2 Corinthians 10:3–5

6. Where does a spirit of oppression attack?

7. What four doors does a spirit of oppression come through against the believer? List them and explain.

CHAPTER 4

STOP OPPOSING YOURSELF

T he Apostle Paul wrote, "For God has not given us a spirit of fear, but of power and of love and of a sound mind" (2 Timothy 1:7, NKJV).

Our God is not responsible for any fear that torments us. We are commanded to reverence and respect God. All other fears are not of God. "For you did not receive a spirit of bondage again to fear, but you received the Sprit of adoption by whom we cry out, '*Abba*, Father'" (Romans 8:15, NKJV).

God has not given us fear. Instead, He has endowed us with power! This power comes not through our own strength, but through His. He has given us the authority to release power in the use of His name. Every believer has this privilege: "These signs will follow those who believe: In My name they will cast out demons" (Mark 16:17, NKJV).

"Cast out" are words of force and authority! You may feel unworthy to use that name above all names because you are deeply oppressed. You may consider yourself the least in the kingdom of heaven. Yet, Jesus said the person least in the kingdom of God is greater than John the Baptist (Matthew 11:11)! How can this be? John the Baptist died before the sacrifice of the Lamb. We, however, have the full benefits of the blood, resurrection, and Lordship of Jesus Christ. We have the victory of the cross! Despite how we think or feel, as children of God, we have power! We have the authority to use the name of Jesus!

Here's what happened when Paul invoked that wonderful name. "Now it happened, as we went to prayer, that a certain slave girl possessed with a spirit of divination met us, who brought her masters much profit by fortune-telling. This girl followed Paul and us, and cried out, saying, 'These men are the servants of the Most High God, who proclaim to us the way of salvation.' And this she did for many days. But Paul, greatly annoyed, turned and said to the spirit, 'I command you in the name of Jesus Christ to come out of her.' And he came out that very hour" (Acts 16:16–18, NKJV).

THE POWER OF JESUS' NAME

What a privilege we have as believers to use that name! It is important to understand the difference between power and authority. A large truck, fully loaded, speeding along the expressway is power in motion. Yet, when the driver sees flashing lights and a badge, he will bring that powerful machine to a stop. The police officer is much smaller and has much less power than the truck, but the badge he wears stands for all the authority of the government it represents. Backed by the law, the police officer has the legal muscle to exercise authority against anyone who violates the law.

Jesus gives his disciples authority over the power of the enemy. "I give you the authority to trample on serpents and scorpions, and over all the power of the enemy, and nothing shall by any means hurt you. Nevertheless do not rejoice in this, that the spirits are subject to you, but rather rejoice because your names are written in heaven" (Luke 10:19–20, NKJV). We do not rejoice because spirits submit to us; rather, we rejoice in the salvation we have obtained through Jesus Christ.

THE POWER OF LOVE

God has given us His love. Love is the power God uses to heal us. "There is no fear in love; but perfect love casts out fear, because fear involves torment. But he who fears has not been made perfect in love" (1 John 4:18, NKJV).

Are you perfect in love? I am not, but God is! He alone will do for us what we cannot do for ourselves, namely, He will "cast out" fear. God will love our hurts away. The greatest healing agent in the world is love!

God has given us a sound mind. Far too many Christians are not in their right minds! They act out of a carnal mind. They live their lives and make decisions based on how they feel instead of the truth of God's Word. Such individuals live in the realm of the soul rather than the spirit. Reason, logic, feelings, and emotions rule their life.

God desires that we have a sound mind. "I beseech you therefore, brethren, by the mercies of God, that you present your bodies a living sacrifice, holy, acceptable to God, which is your reasonable service. And do not be conformed to this world, but be transformed by the renewing of your mind, that you may prove what is that good and acceptable and perfect will of God" (Romans 12:1–2, NKJV).

The mind is renewed by the Word of God. Ephesians 5:26 says He will sanctify and cleanse us "with the washing of water by the Word" (NKJV). In Psalm 119:11, David wrote, "Your word I have hidden in my heart, that I might not sin against You" (NKJV).

When we are not living our lives based upon the Word of God, it is then we begin to stray from truth. Our thinking becomes distorted and contaminated. We take on the world's faulty logic and ideology. God's Word is like a plumb line. It reveals anything as crooked that does not line up to the certainty of truth.

Sometimes, we simply cannot "see" the truth of God's Word for our life. Perhaps ignorance or willful unbelief has blinded us to God's higher reality and purpose. We struggle endlessly, thrashing about to free ourselves of hurt, but no amount of effort affords escape or relief. Then, it becomes necessary to submit to a servant of the Lord for help.

As we truthfully examine the issues facing us with an anointed servant, the Lord will provide new insight and instruction. Insight will help us see the problem as God sees it. We will understand the steps we took in error, away from truth. And God will instruct us how to move towards Him, and into healing restoration.

> "And the servant of the Lord must not strive; but be gentle unto all men, apt to teach, patient, in meekness **instructing those who oppose them-selves**; if God peradventure will give them repentance to

the acknowledging of the truth; and that they may recover themselves out of the snare of the devil, who are taken captive by him at his will" (2 Timothy 2:24–26, KJV).

Turning to another for help requires humility! We must come to the end of ourselves. We must be sick and tired of being sick and tired. We must acknowledge that we have a need, and that we have exhausted our own abilities to correct it. We must be desperate for change. In that attitude, we act in faith. We approach an anointed servant of the Lord as coming to the Lord Himself. "Is anyone among you sick? Let him call for the elders of the church, and let them pray over him, anointing him with oil in the name of the Lord. And the prayer of faith shall save the sick, and the Lord will raise him up. And if he has committed sins, he will be forgiven. Confess your trespasses to one another, and pray for one another, that you may be healed. The effective, fervent prayer of a righteous man avails much" (James 5:14–16, NKVJ).

THE POWER OF CONFRONTATION

How would you like to have Jacob as a son-in-law or as a brother? I could imagine his constant plotting to take advantage of you! He might cook a wonderful dinner of beans for you, then steal your inheritance at the same time. You could never lower your guard! Jacob's name means "supplanter."

Genesis 32 records the story of an important night in Jacob's life. At that moment, he was returning home after many years. The next morning, he was to face his brother who had threatened to kill him.

Alone in the camp, the Angel of the Lord came, in the form of a man, and wrestled with him. The Man asked Jacob, "What is your name?" Why is that significant? The Angel knew Jacob's name meant "supplanter," but Jacob needed to recognize it, too. Jacob's worst enemy wasn't Esau; it was Jacob himself! He could not blame what he had become on family members or anyone else. He alone was responsible for his actions. Change would not occur until he had confronted who he was.

The important truth is this: We must confront offenders. Sometimes that offender is us, and sometimes we are victims of the sins of others. Victims of rape, violence, divorce, abandonment, trauma, and spoken curses can rarely go forward in life as long as they allow the effects of these events from the past to dictate their present. We must be willing to turn loose of the past. If we do not, people from our past will rob us of peace in the present. Some of our offenders may be in the grave, but the memory of that person and what they did holds us prisoner. We must confront the offender, break the curse, and walk free of our prison.

"For we do not wrestle against flesh and blood, but against principalities, against powers, against the rulers of the darkness of this age, against spiritual hosts of wickedness in the heavenly places" (Ephesians 6:12, NKJV).

People are not the problem. A nagging or bitter wife is not the problem. An abusive or absent husband is not the problem. An arrogant or harassing boss is not the problem. *Flesh and blood is not the problem.* People are yielding to, being influenced and manipulated by, *a spirit.* It is this spirit we must confront and defeat!

Peter is an example of how one may be manipulated. "From that time Jesus began to show His disciples that He must go to Jerusalem, and suffer many things from the elders and chief priests and scribes, and be killed, and be raised again the third day. Then Peter took Him aside and began to rebuke Him, saying, 'Far be it from you, Lord; this shall not happen to You!' But He turned and said to Peter, 'Get behind Me, Satan! You are an offense to Me, for you are not mindful of the things of God, but the things of men'" (Matthew 16:21–23, NKJV).

Was Peter full of the devil? Certainly not. Satan had already attempted to thwart the crucifixion by the temptation of Jesus in the wilderness. The words Peter spoke against God's plan for redeeming mankind, intended to influence or tempt Jesus to turn aside from the divine mission. Satan used Peter as an instrument to sabotage the plan of God.

Either we will remain a victim or become a victor over our past. The victim will focus on the offense and the offender. The victor will confront the issue in light of the truth of God's Word, and will receive counsel, comfort, and healing from it.

We cannot change the person or event that brought emotional pain into our life. We can, however, change how we have responded to those issues. The true enemy is *us*. For Jacob the problem was not Abraham, Isaac, Rebekah or Esau. The problem was *Jacob*. When Jacob was willing to confess his name to the Angel, things forever changed.

THE POWER OF INSTRUCTION

"In meekness instructing them that oppose themselves" (2 Timothy 2:25, KJV). Instruction is needed because people "oppose themselves."

Why do we oppose ourselves? We have been programmed with a belief system that will always bring self-defeat. Traumatic events of the past and the emotional pain those events have caused open our mind to our spiritual enemy. Satan's distorted, deceiving whispers enter our thoughts, and we believe them. We believe we are to blame, that we are inferior, without purpose and hope. To cope, we change our behavior. We hide from others behind a façade of smiles, or we retreat into the darkness of isolation.

A demonic spirit cannot possess a born-again Christian. However, a demonic assignment does not change simply because one is a believer. Man is the only creation made in the image of God. It is Satan's deviant passion to destroy anything God places value on. Our physical body is targeted by Satan because it was made in the image of God.

> ...a demonic assignment does not change simply because one is a believer.

If a spirit cannot possess a body, it attempts to manipulate the body. Consequently, we are instructed: "do not let sin reign in your mortal body, that you should obey it in its lusts. And do not present your members as instruments of unrighteousness to sin, but present yourself to God as being alive from the dead, and your members as instruments of righteousness to God." (Romans 6:12–13, NKJV). This implies we have a will and a choice about the control of our body. We must not present it to the control of sin by our willful actions. We must yield ourselves to the spirit for righteousness.

Comedian Flip Wilson once made us laugh by excusing his self-indulgent actions with, "The devil made me do it!" But James 1:14 says sin is a choice: "Each one is tempted when he is drawn away by his own desires and enticed" (NKJV) Satan cannot force us to sin; rather, he can and does entice us to use our body for sinful purposes.

When we present our body for sinful purposes, we become our own worst enemy. We "oppose ourselves" in the pursuit of our spiritual purpose.

Eventually, the pain we feel in our emotions and our familiar pattern of reacting to it creates harmful habits. We become "locked in" to damaging actions when confronted by familiar situations. For instance, a person attempting to stop smoking will, after a meal, habitually reach for the pocket where cigarettes have been kept in the past. The person may certainly know the pocket is empty, but habit dictates the response.

A spirit of oppression will entice with the intent of manipulating us to use our body to sin. A person manipulated by fear may be timid, withdrawn, and introverted. The body will react by averting the eyes when addressed by another person. The individual will sit alone in a crowd and avoid conversation that gives insight to his hurt.

A person with anger issues is enticed to "blow his top." He is predisposed to say something hurtful or cutting, or even to slap or to hit his adversary. If he yields to such temptation, he has used his body as an instrument of unrighteousness.

One of my closest friends had predictable behavior. He was a born-again Christian and successful, but he was tormented. Once a month he would relive the molestation of his childhood. He would sit by the hour in a rocking chair and walk through self-inflicted torment. He never felt he was good enough to be worthy of his many blessings. He mourned over his past, and did not allow himself to be affectionate with his family.

His family lived with fear while he worked through those days of torment. They shared the misery with him! He would not talk to anyone. During his depression, there was not joy in the house. Mentally, he took out the chains of his past and beat himself.

THE POWER OF CONFESSION

Our key verse, 2 Timothy 2:25, concludes with an interesting statement: "In meekness instructing those that oppose themselves; **if God peradventure will give them repentance to the acknowledging of the truth**" (KJV).

The motive for instruction is to bring change. The Word of God will always find lodging. Like other seeds, the seed of the Word will bring a positive result, even though it may require time to germinate and become visible.

Repentance means "to have change of mind." Remember that the mind must be renewed by the Word of God. Our problem is that we have opinions that we believe to be truth when they are not. "There is a way *that seems* right to a man, but its end *is* the way of death" (Proverbs 14:12, NKJV).

We must forego our opinion for the truth of God's Word. What God is seeking through the instruction of the Word is the acknowledgement of truth. He desires that we stop speaking our opinion about the issue and begin confessing what His Word has to say about the matter.

Nothing is going to change when I address oppression with my counsel and wisdom. But when I speak His Word to the mountain, it will be removed and cast into the sea. When I react according to the Word of God, change will occur. The truth will make us free. If I believe and confess what the Word says about my issue tomorrow and each day thereafter, I will be free. But the day I do not believe the truth I receive and put it to practice immediately, I will begin to regress into oppression.

WHOSE BATTLE IS IT?

Too often a person seeking help with emotional healing is looking for a quick fix. He wants someone to lay hands on him so he can be healed in seconds from a lifetime of emotional damage and pain.

God has provided for us all the weapons of warfare necessary to defeat our enemy. The victory is the Lord's, but the battle is ours. When David was told to go into battle, the Lord promised victory, yet David and his army had to fight. Jesus has done His part. He sacrificially died for us. He was raised from the dead. Now we must do our part to assure victory.

"Having these promises, beloved, let us cleanse ourselves from all filthiness of the flesh and spirit, perfecting holiness in the fear of God" (2 Corinthians 7:1, NKJV). What a marvelous hope and encouragement! We may recover ourselves! Change is possible! The oppression can stop!

"That they may recover themselves out of the snare of the devil, who are taken captive by him at his will" (2 Timothy 2:26, KJV).

The words "snare" and "captive" in this verse create a picture in the mind. "Snare" gives the impression that one is trapped, struggling to be free. "Captive" suggests one being imprisoned against his will.

Who has cast the snare? Who takes us captive? The devil. Take note of the words "captive by him to do his will." What is this if not manipulation?

Imagine a conversation between evil spirits of oppression. One says, "Watch this! I can make him curse when he is angry!" The other says, "Watch this! I can make him have such fear he will cry endlessly." Another says, "Watch this! I can make him smoke when he feels anxious."

Demonic manipulation appears similar to a puppet on a string. Observers see only the puppet's natural movements; they do not see the hands that pull the strings. A scent, a picture, a place—an insignificant thing or event—can trigger a memory that causes us to act out in a predictable fashion.

Behavioral habits may be broken. Reaction habits may be broken. They are broken as we apply the truth of God's Word, and cease opposing ourselves.

CHAPTER FOUR
DISCUSSION QUESTIONS

1. According to 2 Timothy 1:7, what has God given us to "stop opposing ourselves"?

2. What is God's element of healing for emotional pain? (pg. 36–37)

3. If a spirit cannot possess a believer's body, what does he attempt to do with it? Explain Romans 6:12. (pg. 40)

4. According to 2 Timothy 2:25, why is instruction necessary? (pg. 40)

5. According to 2 Timothy 2:26, who is going to deliver you out of the snare?

6. Explain the power of "acknowledging" the truth in 2 Timothy 2:26.

CHAPTER 5

WHAT MUST I SURRENDER TO BE FREE?

Margie is a strong willed, controlling person. She has been hurt deeply and rebels against any form of authority. No one is going to tell her what to do. From the outset of our prayer session, she was guarded and made every attempt to be in control of everything said to her.

At a certain point in the session, Margie was asked to surrender control and forgive those who had hurt her. Using Jesus and Stephen the martyr as examples, we encouraged her to offer the same prayer of forgiveness: "Father, forgive them, for they do not know what they are doing."

Immediately, she shut down and pulled back. Her thought was easy to determine. *I'm not Jesus; I will never be Jesus; and I'm not going to forgive and forget.* Needless to say, we were very limited in our attempt to help her. She left disappointed and unchanged.

We make a choice. We can wrestle against flesh and blood and continue to be oppressed, or we can surrender to the truth. "For our struggle is not against flesh and blood, but against the rulers, against the authorities, against the powers of this dark world and against spiritual forces of evil in the heavenly realms" (Ephesians 6:12, NIV).

Emotional healing will occur quickly when one surrenders two things: unforgiveness and control.

FORGIVENESS IS REQUIRED

Forgiveness is a requirement to emotional healing. When we have been hurt deeply, forgiveness requires more than just saying, "Okay, I forgive." Most likely, this is a feeble attempt at avoiding the past in an effort to get on with my life. Usually, we have not truly forgiven, and have suppressed our true feelings that will surface again at a later time.

Forgiveness is a process. It requires a daily confrontation of our hurt and emotions. This releases a person from our debt, and allows "bringing every though into captivity to the obedience of Christ, and being ready to punish all disobedience when our obedience is fulfilled" (2 Corinthians 10:5–6, NKJV).

Our own forgiveness is based upon the condition of our forgiving others. It is commanded of us. "For if you forgive men their trespasses, your heavenly Father will also forgive you. But if you do not forgive men their trespasses, neither will your Father forgive your trespasses" (Matthew 6:14–15, NKJV).

There are twelve inches between heaven and hell—the distance from the head to the heart. To forgive from the heart brings release and healing. To choose not to forgive gives the enemy an open door to continue his torment and interference in our life.

Jesus told this story:

"Then his master, after he had called him, said to him, 'You wicked servant! I forgave you all that debt because you begged me. Should you not also have had compassion on your fellow servant, just as I had pity on you?' And his master was angry, and delivered him to the torturers until he should pay all that was due to him. So My heavenly Father also will do to you if each of you, **from his heart**, does not forgive his brother his trespasses" (Matthew 18:32–35, NKJV).

The Lord makes it clear to us that forgiveness must be from the heart.

The blessing of giving forgiveness is that we are forgiven when we forgive others. The penalty of not forgiving others is to remain guilty before God. If we do not forgive, we cannot be forgiven.

The person or persons responsible for our emotional pain may never change their attitude or behavior. They may continue to treat us in the same manner they always have. We cannot change them, but we can release ourselves from the snare of the devil through the healing power of forgiveness.

"Then Peter came to Him and said, 'Lord, how often shall my brother sin against me, and I forgive him? Up to seven times?' Jesus said to him, 'I do not say to you, up to seven times, but up to seventy times seven'" (Matthew 18:21–22, NKJV).

What God demands of us, He Himself does by example: "I will forgive their iniquity, and their sin I will remember no more" (Jeremiah 31:34, NKJV). David wrote that He forgives all our iniquities
(Psalm 103:3).

God chooses to forgive. Likewise, forgiveness is a choice for us, as well. We are to forgive when asked. "Take heed to yourselves. If your brother sins against you, rebuke him; and if he repents, forgive him. And if he sins against you seven times in a day, and seven times in a day returns to you, saying 'I repent,' you shall forgive him" (Luke 17:3–4, NKJV).

We are to forgive when forgiveness isn't requested. We are never more like Jesus than when we choose to forgive. Jesus prayed from the cross, "Father, forgive them for they do not know what they are doing" (Luke 23:34, NIV). Stephen, the first martyr in the book of Acts, prayed: "Lord, do not hold this sin against them" (Acts 7:60, NIV)

God would not have commanded us to forgive if it was impossible to fulfill it.

In my late forties, the Lord confronted me concerning my own issues with unforgiveness. My experiences in church were not always pleasant. During my childhood years, I witnessed a great deal of hypocrisy and legalism. This legalism robbed me of the joy of being a teenager. Being a minister's son placed me in a position of having to live at a higher standard than other youth in the church. I also became increasingly bitter seeing my father in anguish as a result of harsh criticism from people who claimed lives of holiness. Later it would be revealed that these people were in gross sin.

I promised myself that when I became an adult I would never again darken a church door. When God called me into ministry, I asked the Lord to help me love people. He promised me He would.

I thought I dealt with the bitterness of past, but I had not. Years later as I went through emotional healing, the moderator confronted me about bitterness that legalism had deposited in my life. She told me I had to forgive people that had hurt me! I laughed out loud because I thought I had dealt with those issues.

Whenever I preached or taught against legalism, people from my past would come to mind. Their memory would trigger a resentment that would express itself in my preaching. Some people may have even mistaken my emotional anger as an anointing.

We have the power to forgive!

It was not the anointing. It was pain being expressed. Then, going through emotional healing, I was asked to forgive. I was shocked to hear myself say, "I am not really sure I want to!" It was then I realized I had buried my pain in an attempt to get on with my life.

Many of the people I needed to forgive were dead. The only way I could "get even" with them was not to forgive them. Then the Lord showed me that by not forgiving, I was allowing dead people affect the peace of my present. I made them prisoners in my mind and would bring them out to punish them for what they had done. But they were not prisoners—I was! I was the one being tormented by the past!

In that moment I understood the power of forgiveness. From my heart, I forgave them of their offenses to me. Immediately I felt as if a thousand pounds had been lifted from me. When I made the decision to release them from the prison I created, I was set free.

The Lord gave us the example of how forgiveness is completed: "their sin I will remember no more" (Jeremiah 31:34, NKJV).

When you read the Old Testament and come across the word "remember," it is usually the Hebrew word *zakar*. The term has a very broad meaning and is sometimes translated as "mention," "recorder," "mindful," "think," "bring to remembrance," and "call to mind." Consequently, forgiving someone completely requires choosing to let go of every aspect of this broad understanding of remember:

1. **We must choose not to focus on the offense any longer.**
By choosing to forgive, we eliminate the destructive power of our past responses, and eliminate the reason for our guilt.

We have the power to forgive!

"Now, regarding the one who started all this—the person in question who caused all this pain—I want you to know that I am not the one injured in this as much as, with a few exceptions, all of you. So I don't want to come down too hard. What the majority of you agreed to as punishment is punishment enough. Now is the time to forgive this man and help him back on his feet. If all you do is pour on guilt, you could very well drown him in it. My counsel now is to pour on the love.

"The focus of my letter wasn't on punishing the offender but on getting you to take responsibility for the health of the church. So if you forgive him, I forgive him." (2 Corinthians 2:5–9, The Message).

The power of forgiveness is to choose love without conditions. When we make this choice, love covers a multitude of sins. We have truly forgiven when we can help the offender back on his feet.

2. **We must refuse to attempt to control the offender by continuing to bring up the past.** We are easily tempted to keep revisiting the past in order to remind a person how badly they acted toward us, and how it hurt us. A husband, wife, son, daughter, or close friend will struggle with resentment if we attempt to control them by bringing up the past.

Such control is not a release of debts. It is not love. The Word informs us that love "doesn't keep score of the sins of others, doesn't revel when others grovel, takes pleasure in the flowering of truth, puts up with anything" (1 Corinthians 13:5–7, The Message).

3. We choose not to inform others about their offense.

One specific concept connected to the Hebrew word *zakar* is "mention," which is easily understandable because mentioning something brings it back to remembrance.

When we speak about an offense, we open a memory and an emotion that we will continue to deal with. If an offense is to heal, we must forgive and not mention it again. When a wound is healing, don't pick the scab!

The purpose behind forgiving is to restore.

Jim Elliot, missionary to Ecuador, said before he was martyred, "A man is no fool who gives up what he cannot keep to gain that which he cannot lose."

> *The purpose behind forgiving is to restore.*

His wife, Elisabeth, and family returned to the country of his martyrdom, and experienced a marvelous harvest. Later, I saw a Billy Graham program with Jim Elliot's son and a strange looking man. He was one of the Aucca Indians responsible for killing Jim! Through the effort of

Elizabeth and children, the man had found Christ. The Elliot's grandchildren called him "papa."

Had they chosen not to forgive, they would have remained prisoners of bitterness. Instead, they chose to love and forgive, thus reaching others in the tribe with the testimony of Jesus. We, too, can forgive!

SURRENDER THE NEED TO CONTROL

When one has suffered emotional pain, a common way of coping is to become a controller. Because of our vulnerability, we build walls around ourselves to protect us from being hurt again.

In time, we become the ones creating pain in the lives of others. It has been said, "hurting people hurt people." Hurting people hurt others because they find it difficult to be open with their feelings. People may not know that our real problem is insecurity because we mask it in order to get our way. To gain control, we may use manipulation, rebellion, anger, or dominance. If we do not get our way, our peace is disturbed.

We may feel the need to be in control because we have been victimized and will not allow ourselves to become vulnerable again. This becomes a major factor in the emotional healing process. Healing cannot come until we are willing to submit.

First and foremost, we are to submit to God. "Therefore submit to God. Resist the devil and he will flee from you" (James 4:7, NKJV). Through submission to God, we gain power and authority to combat the forces of Satan. Through submission, we acknowledge we are helpless and not self-sufficient. The Father waits for us to end our own efforts. By relying on Him, He empowers us to resist the devil.

We are not only to submit to God, but also to man. "Yes, all of you be submissive to one another, and be clothed with humility, for 'God resists the proud, but gives grace to the humble'" (1 Peter 5:5, NKJV).

Our healing will not come until we get exasperated with our attempts to heal ourselves. We need God's help, and we need the body of Christ.

In his epistle, James addressed this very issue. He wrote, "Is anyone among you sick? Let him call for the elders of the church, and let them pray over him, anointing him with oil in the name of the Lord. And the prayer of faith will save the sick, and the Lord will raise him up. And if he has committed sins, he will be forgiven. Confess your trespasses to one another, and pray for one another, that you may be healed" (James 5:14–16, NKJV).

Healing will come when we openly submit ourselves to one another. We take a major step when we reveal to another believer our sins and sufferings.

A person experiencing great emotional pain and oppression often does not feel secure talking about what has happened to him. He has not given himself permission to talk about it. He feels no one else has had such an experience, so no one would understand. He may also conclude that if another person found out about his secret, that person would not like him.

It is my experience that people feel an immediate sense of relief through sharing their traumatic experience with someone. Dr. Berl Best, former counselor at Central Bible College in Springfield, Missouri, informed me that the more a person shares what has happened to him, the more quickly he can recover from this pain.

A person came to me for emotional healing who experienced a great deal of trauma in his life. This person had become very dominant and controlling. He had been treated for a bi-polar condition and diagnosed as paranoid schizophrenic. The emotional pain was so intense that he had been cutting himself and had attempted suicide.

I explained that forgiveness and release of control were necessary before healing would occur. The person immediately confessed his dominance and weariness from the pain it was bringing others. When I started the session, we immediately began to confront a haughty spirit before going to any other stronghold. This had to be broken first.

After teaching about this stronghold, I laid my hands on the man's head and began to take authority over the haughty spirit. The power of God's Word immediately broke the stronghold. Those of us present with him were shocked when he began to regurgitate.

This happened every time we prayed against any stronghold we knew this person was dealing with. It was eye opening, to say the least!

This was the first time I had witnessed such a manifestation, but would see it many times afterward. Healing came quickly because the person exercised his willingness to submit to God and His Word.

CHAPTER FIVE
DISCUSSION QUESTIONS

---

1. What two things must be surrendered for rapid emotional healing to occur? (pg. 46, 50)

2. What is the difference between forgiving from the head and from the heart? Explain.

3. How is forgiveness a process?

4. List three things that will indicate a person has truly forgiven.

5. What are some reasons a person may refuse to release control?

CHAPTER 6

FIGHTING A TERRORIST

The nations of the world are in total unrest because of terrorism. Scores of zealous young men and women have been trained to kill in ways designed to maximize chaos and mass destruction. The successful attack on the World Trade Center in New York City on September 11, 2001, forever changed the peace and security of America. A few terrorists, united in their malicious intent and supported by outside religious fundamentalists, struck a savage blow against the country's tranquility, and almost brought the American economy to its knees.

Terrorists are so driven by their radical beliefs they will sacrifice their own lives to destroy anyone who does not espouse their views. They have set their mind and will to annihilate opposing religions or ideology. This deception and violence is demonically inspired.

In the same manner, Satan and his army are just as intent on attacking the peace and borders of your life. Jesus warned that "the thief does not come except to steal, and to kill, and to destroy. I have come that they may have life, and that they may have it more abundantly" (John 10:10, NKJV).

When you understand your enemy, the access he had in your life, the destruction he caused, and his plan of attack, you are neither defenseless nor helpless!

Just as an army has a strategy and tactics for dealing with terrorists, we, too, have means of dealing with our enemy. Ralph Peter's book, *When Devils Walk the Earth*, lists ideas for dealing successfully with terrorists. These principles also apply to dealing with a spirit of oppression or possession, whichever we may encounter.

1. Be feared.
Instead of being a victim of fear, become the one to be feared. You have the authority of Jesus' name, the power of the blood, the Word of God, and the Holy Spirit. You are the devil's nightmare. You have been released with an anointing to expand God's kingdom in the same manner as Jesus' disciples. He sent them out two-by-two and gave them power over demons and diseases. They came back rejoicing because demons were subject to them! Jesus told them, "I give you the authority to trample on serpents and scorpions, and over all the power of

the enemy, and nothing shall by any means hurt you" (Luke 10:19, NKJV).

We must know that we are more than conquerors through Jesus Christ. When we fully understand and are convinced that we are mighty through God, we are well on our way to being feared by our enemy.

2. Identify the type of terrorist you face, and know your enemy as well as possible.

We must study the methods, movements, manifestations of Satan and his cohorts, and be familiar with the words he uses to oppress.

Demonic activity in our life must be destroyed, not tolerated. We have not obtained victory until we have completely dealt with it. We must have no tolerance for allowing it to continue. We cannot hope for success if we remove only part of a tumor; we must remove all of it!

3. Do not be afraid to be powerful.

"You are of God, little children, and have overcome them, because He who is in you is greater than he who is in the world" (1 John 4:4, NKJV).

The armor of the Lord is not just for defense, but also offense:

> "Therefore take up the whole armor of God, that you may be able to withstand in the evil day, and having done all, to stand.

Stand, therefore, having girded your waist truth, having put on the breastplate of righteousness, and having shod your feet with the preparation of the gospel of peace; above all, taking the shield of faith with which you will be able to quench all the fiery darts of the wicked one. And take the helmet of salvation, and the sword of the Spirit, which is the word of God, praying always with all prayer and supplication in the Spirit, being watchful to this end with all perseverance and supplication for all the saints" (Ephesians 6:13–18, NKJV).

When we fail to use this armor, we contribute to our own defeat.

4. Speak bluntly.
Timid speech leads to timid actions. Speak of *killing* terrorists and *destroying* their organizations. Our conversation should be filled with confidence. Our words must be authoritative, never apologetic.

When David faced Goliath, he spoke with authority:

"Then David said to the Philistine, 'You come to me with a sword, with a spear, and with a javelin. But I come to you in the name of the Lord of hosts, the God of the armies of Israel, whom you have defied.

This day the Lord will deliver you into my hand, and I will strike you and take your head from you. And this day I will give the carcasses of the camp of the Philistines to the birds of the air and the wild beasts of the earth, that all the earth may know that there is a God in Israel. Then all this assembly shall know that the Lord does not save with sword and spear; for the battle *is* the LORD's, and He will give you into our hands.'" (1 Samuel 17:45–47, NKJV).

Once again, Jesus gives us an example for addressing our enemy. In Mark 1:25, Jesus rebuked an evil spirit and commanded him to be quiet. The NIV records that Jesus spoke "sternly."

Too many Christians treat the enemy like an annoying dog that nips at their ankles. They speak to him in a whining voice, "Get away." But when they have had enough of the dog's disruptive behavior, they slap their hands together, stoop over as if to grab the dog, and with a stern voice command him to "Get!" We must command with confidence and authority!

During the emotional healing process, when one is rebuking a spirit of oppression, it is not loudness, but, rather, knowing who you are in Christ and speaking the Word of God with boldness and authority that intimidates our enemy.

5. Concentrate on winning the propaganda war where it is winnable.

The devil wants to taunt and intimidate you publicly. He wants to challenge your character and self-esteem. For good reason he is called the "accuser of the brethren." He speaks words to you intending to destroy your faith. Goliath is such an example.

> "And the Philistine said, 'I defy the armies of Israel this day; give me a man that we may fight together.' When Saul and all Israel heard these words of the Philistine, they were dismayed and greatly afraid" (1 Samuel 17:10–11, NKJV).

Goliath's words had turned the king of Israel into a coward and made the armies of Israel weak. They were helpless because of the words of the giant.

Goliath attempted to instill fear in David:

> "And when the Philistine looked about and saw David, he disdained him; for he was only a youth, ruddy and good-looking. So the Philistine said to David, 'Am I a dog, that you come to me with sticks?' And the Philistine cursed David by his gods. And the Philistine said to David, 'Come to me, and I will give your flesh to the birds of the air and the beasts of the fields!'" (1 Samuel 17:42–44, NKJV).

The propaganda war is won by preaching, teaching, praying, and speaking the Word of God when encountering a challenge from the enemy. The devil is "the accuser of our brethren" (Revelation 12:10, NKJV).

My uncle, Houston Johnson, was a Nazarene pastor until he died. Shortly after I married, my wife and I moved next door to him. As he was concluding an evening walk, I asked him what he had been up to, and he said, "I've been out all day slandering the devil because I know he is doing the same to me!"

Our assignment is to place the name of Jesus—who He is and what He has done—before as many people as we possibly can. The confession of our mouth is not only a part of our initial salvation experience, but it guarantees our victory over Satan. "They overcame him by the blood of the Lamb and by the word of their testimony" (Revelation 12:11, NKJV).

We must make known the power of Jesus over Satan! The devil has been overselling himself! He wants us to believe he is omnipresent, omnipotent, and omniscient. In truth, all these are lies. He is a created being, a fallen angel with no hope of forgiveness with God, and the father of lies. He has been defeated by the sinless, life resurrection, and authority of Jesus Christ, the Son of God. Satan is under the feet of Jesus and our feet, as well (Romans 16:20).

6. Do not be drawn into a public dialog with terrorists.

Whenever demons began to speak in the presence of Jesus, He rebuked them and cast them out! Attempting to have a conversation with a spirit serves no purpose. If a spirit manifests, it is because a righteous person is present and the Lord wants the stronghold broken.

Paul provides us an example.

"This girl followed Paul and us, and cried out, saying, 'These men are the servants of the Most High God, who proclaim to us the way of salvation.' And this she did for many days. But Paul, greatly annoyed, turned and said to the spirit, 'I command you in the name of Jesus Christ to come out of her.' And he came out that very hour" (Acts 16:17–18, NKJV).

The best means of dealing with the terrorist is to ignore his accusations and silence him.

7. Avoid those who compete for attention and have agendas, often selfish.

When confronting our enemy in spiritual warfare, there are those who may be involved with the process whose motives are not pure. They may be jealous of how God uses you.

In the book of Acts, when Phillip took the gospel to Samaria, a great revival broke out. A man who had been used as a sorcerer was converted. When Peter and John were sent from Jerusalem to help in the move of God, they laid hands on people to receive the Holy Spirit. Simon, the sorcerer, wanted power to do the same, and offered money to obtain it. He was jealous of what God was doing through these apostles.

> "And when Simon saw that through the laying on of the apostles' hands the Holy Spirit was given, he offered them money, saying, 'Give me this power also, that anyone on whom I lay my hands may receive the Holy Spirit.' But Peter said to him, 'Your money perish with you, because you thought that the gift of God could be purchased with money! You have neither part nor portion in this matter, for your heart is not right in the sight of God'" (Acts 8:18–21, NKJV).

Any person helping with the emotional healing or deliverance process that is lacking pure motives should be confronted. That person becomes a hindrance to God's purpose.

When David was about to confront Goliath, his oldest brother Eliab accused him of coming to the battle with wrong motives. In reality Eliab, motivated by jealously, was used in an attempt to dishearten the man God had already anointed as the next king of Israel. It was a satanic strategy to keep David out of the battle. David's pure heart and zeal for God deflected Eliab's discouraging words, and won a great victory for Israel.

8. Maintain Resolve.

We must apply constant pressure to the enemy. We must make him aware of our intentions to never waver or let up.

9. When in doubt, hit harder than you think necessary.

Maximum force should be used at the beginning of a battle. When the United States invaded Iraq, the strategy was to overwhelm the enemy with a show of great force dubbed "Shock and Awe."

When Israel miraculously crossed the Red Sea, word spread concerning the power of the God of Israel. Later, spies who entered Jericho for surveillance were given a hiding place in the home of Rahab, a harlot. Listen to Rahab's confession:

> "I know that the Lord has given you the land, that the terror of you has fallen on us, and that all the inhabitants of the land are fainthearted because of you. For we have heard how the Lord dried up the water of the Red Sea for you when you came out of Egypt, and what you did to the two kings of the Amorites who were on the other side

of the Jordan, Sihon and Og, whom you utterly destroyed. And as soon as we heard these things, our hearts melted; neither did there remain any more courage in anyone because of you, for the Lord your God, He is God in heaven above and on earth beneath" (Joshua 2:9–11, NKJV).

Use such dynamic power that it stuns the enemy! Prayer support should not come in the middle or at the end of a life crisis, but rather, at the slightest hint of trouble. Praying in the Spirit, agreeing in faith, maintaining unity of purpose, and allowing no compromise of truth intimidates the enemy.

10. Kill a terrorist on the spot. Do not give him a chance to surrender.

This is war, not law enforcement.

"I will send My fear before you, I will cause confusion among all the people to whom you come, and will make all your enemies turn their backs to you" (Exodus 23:27, NKJV).

"Now go and attack Amalek, and utterly destroy all that they have, and do not spare them. But kill both man and woman, infant and nursing child, ox and sheep, camel and donkey" (1 Samuel 15:3, NKJV).

God's instruction made certain that there would be no survivor to avenge, or take up the cause, of their family. For a similar reason, presumptuous kings often killed all rival heirs to the throne.

Sin not dealt with, or character issues not confronted, will continue to cause pain and personal destruction. A flaw that was once small and non-threatening, if allowed to continue, will overwhelm you in the end.

The life of Samson teaches us this valuable lesson.

> "Samson went down to Timnah together with his father and mother. As they approached the vineyards of Timnah, suddenly a young lion came roaring toward him. The Spirit of the Lord came upon him in power so that he tore the lion apart with his bare hands as he might have torn a young goat" (Judges 14:5–6, NIV).

I believe that vineyard represents the favor, abundance, and promises of God. Satan attacks when we set our mind to go after the blessings of God.

When Samson was attacked, "the Spirit of the Lord came upon him in power." We, too, have access this power through God's Spirit in us. By relying on the Holy Spirit, our battles can also result in amazing victories. This results in incredible encouragement and readiness for future battles because we have experienced victory over our enemies by the power of God.

11. Do not allow a terrorist to hide behind religion.

Legalism is destructive because it places guilt and insecurity in a believer's life. In the name of religion, the Pharisees put heavy burdens and restrictions on those who followed their teachings. These teachings did not reflect the true heart of God. Instead, they created guilt and sorrow in those who sincerely strove to please God, but fell short because of these man-imposed regulations.

In this way, the devil, as an angel of light, uses seducing spirits to pervert the truth of the gospel. Such doctrines of devils must be confronted with the truth of God's Word.

Terrorists want to rob us of our peace and the relationship we have with our Father. Through legalism, serving Jesus freely is not possible. Peter gives a clear explanation as to what occurs when one attempts to live by rules of religion.

"After much discussion, Peter got up and addressed them: 'Brothers, you know that some time ago God made a choice among you that the Gentiles might hear from my lips the message of the gospel and believe.

God, who knows the heart, showed that He accepted them by giving the Holy Spirit to them, just as He did to us. He made no distinction between us and them, for he purified their hearts by faith. Now then, **why do you try to test God by putting on the necks of the disciples a yoke that neither we nor our fathers have been able to bear?** No! We believe it is through the grace of our Lord Jesus that we are saved, just as they are'" (Acts 15:7–11, NIV).

Freedom from religion comes when we do not attempt to please God out of fleshly efforts. We are not saved "by works of righteousness which we have done, but according to His mercy He saved us (Titus 3:5, NKJV). We are to live life freely by "growing in grace and knowledge of the truth."

12. Do not allow a terrorist sanctuary in any place, at any time.

"Give no place to the devil," the Bible instructs. Tobiah and Sanballet opposed Nehemiah when he was rebuilding the wall in Jerusalem. They made every effort to stop the work from being completed. Upon completion of the project, Nehemiah returned to serve the king. Later, he made a second trip to Jerusalem and examined the progress of the city.

"I came to Jerusalem and discovered the evil that Eliashib had done for Tobiah, in preparing a room for him in the courts of the house of God. And it grieved me bitterly; therefore I threw all the household goods of Tobiah out of the room. Then I commanded them to cleanse the rooms; and I brought back into them the articles of the house of God, with the grain offerings and the frankincense." (Nehemiah 13:7–9, NKJV).

The man who had opposed the work so vehemently was residing in the courts of the house of God! We are the temple of the Holy Spirit. We must not allow our enemy to store his goods in our heart. We must rid ourselves of him and purify our hearts.

CHAPTER SIX
DISCUSSION QUESTIONS

---

1. How is a satanic attack like a terrorist? (pg. 54)

2. How do you make war against a spiritual terrorist? (pg. 55)

3. What mentality are we to have that will bring fear to the enemy? (pg. 55)

4. How is the "propaganda war" won? (pg. 58)

5. What does the Bible mean when it says "Give no place to the devil"?

6. What does religious legalism place on the believer? What does legalism take from the believer? (pg. 62)

7. How do we break free from religion? (pg. 62)

CHAPTER 7

OUT OF THE SNARE

L isa Eads is a nurse who attends our church. For several weeks, I shared the truth concerning strongholds and emotional healing in our Sunday night services. She was there the night I preached on a spirit of infirmity. Lisa had spent several thousand dollars on medical tests, only to be frustrated with no diagnosis. Test results were negative. As she recognized the stronghold in her life and began applying the truth of God's Word, immediately the sickness ceased. Lisa gave a public testimony that God had delivered her from physical pain as she took authority over a spirit of infirmity.

Applying the authority of God's Word is powerful! It is the Word of God that renews our mind (Romans 12:2). It is the truth that sets us free (John 8:32).

We must fill our mind with the Word by studying and memorizing it. As a child, I heard cursing and foul talking from both sides of my family. Those words played endlessly in my mind, and I was unable to stop them. I gave my heart to Jesus when I was five, but I sat in an eighth grade Civics class with those curse words swirling in my head. Bowing my head, I prayed silently for God to take away those evil thoughts.

I got the idea to sing "Amazing Grace" and quote every scripture I had memorized. So I did, and the words left!

I came to realize I could not think two thoughts at the same time. By submitting my thoughts to the Word of God, tormenting words found no place. The Apostle Paul said as much in Philippians 4:8–9:

> "Finally, brothers, whatever is true, whatever is noble, whatever is right, whatever is pure, whatever is lovely, whatever is admirable—if anything is excellent or praiseworthy—think about such things. Whatever you have learned or received or heard from me, or seen in me—put into practice. And the God of peace will be with you" (NIV).

Whenever I speak of this event in my life, those ugly words present themselves to my mind. When they do, I speak the Word of God aloud or begin to praise and thank God. When I act in my will, using the authority of God's Word, those words flee.

In Matthew 4, Jesus was tempted by the devil. He quoted three verses from Deuteronomy, and Satan left him. The more knowledge and revelation of Scripture we have in our mind, the greater the weapon we have at our disposal. The more we give place to the Holy Spirit, the more freedom we enjoy. "Where the Spirit of the Lord is, there is freedom" (2 Corinthians 3:17, NIV).

So put the Word in your mind and cultivate a relationship with Him. By walking in the Spirit, we can overcome the snares of the enemy. We can bring our carnal nature into subjection. This is the greatest area of vulnerability in a believer.

What are the characteristics of a carnal nature? Find them in Galatians 5:19–21: "Sexual immorality, impurity and debauchery; idolatry and witchcraft; hatred, discord, jealousy, fits of rage, selfish ambition, dissensions, factions and envy; drunkenness, orgies, and the like. I warn you, as I did before, that those who live like this will not inherit the kingdom of God" (NIV).

The Holy Spirit will take us to the cross. There, we must confront and put to death our passions and desires. How is this possible? By the power of the Holy Spirit. This is not the power of the human spirit, but, rather, the power of the Holy

Spirit. "If by the Spirit you put to death the misdeeds of the body, you will live" (Romans 8:13, NKJV).

Forgiveness received or given has the power to heal!

If we mortify the deeds of the body and begin to walk in the Spirit, the stronghold of the enemy is destroyed. The enemy's hold begins to slip, and we have confidence that our behavior and desires are changed to afford blessings and peace. Love, joy, peace, goodness, faithfulness, gentleness, and self-control begin to govern our life.

When we die with Christ at the cross, so will the emotions generated by our past. A dead man does not have feelings! Offenses committed against us are buried at Calvary.

RELEASE THE POWER OF FORGIVENESS

Next, we must exercise our will to forgive those who are responsible for our emotional pain, including ourselves. If we can surrender the offense to Jesus, we can also release the offender.

Julie Ballard lost her sister Shelly in a tragic accident. At age 7, Shelly was stepping away from a school bus when the bus driver failed to see her.

Shelly was struck and killed. For twenty-five years, Julie felt that a part of her had been lost. It troubled her that the bus driver, a woman, never contacted her to express remorse. Touched by the Holy Spirit, Julie made a decision to reach out to the driver. She tried to call the woman, but had to settle for a conversation with her son. As Julie related her feelings to the man, she asked him to inform his mother that she had come to grips with Shelly's death. God, and she, wanted the bus driver to know that nothing was done that required forgiveness. The bus driver was not responsible for life or death; only God could decide that issue.

The driver's son began to weep over the phone. He said, "You don't know what your words will mean to my mom. She has been so ashamed, so grieved and overwhelmed with guilt all these years. The ridicule and resentment from the community kept her from leaving the house. You just don't know what this will mean to her!"

Forgiveness received or given has the power to heal!

We may choose to forgive, but fear how our offender will respond to us afterward. The people we forgive may not change the way they treat us, but we must change our attitude towards them. Jesus and Stephen both prayed that God would forgive the ones responsible for taking their lives. We must likewise forgive in the same manner, from the heart.

Forgiveness must be ongoing! It cannot be just for the moment. We must walk in love towards our offender. We must guard ourselves with love so as not to be offended again by any new actions towards us.

Our posture must not be like that of a certain father with his son. One day the father tightened his arm muscle and told his son to "Give me your best shot!" The teen did! The blow stung, but the father laughed and shrugged it off. "Is that all you've got?" he asked.

A few days later, the two walked together down a city street when the son decided to play the game again—but this time without the invitation from his dad. "I wonder what Dad will do if I hit him when he isn't ready?" the young man thought. He sent a powerful blow to his unsuspecting and unprepared father. The older man reacted instinctively. Without thinking, he spun around and whacked his son hard on the shoulder.

What made the father react and hit his son? He was not prepared for the hit! He was caught off guard! To walk in forgiveness, we must always be prepared for unsuspecting blows. We must raise a guard of love.

We must forgive unconditionally, too. Consider the way most parents love their children. Even though a son may rebel, break their hearts, even turn to crime, parents will never stop loving him. Yet, the hurts and emotions that surface during the ordeal may influence the husband and wife to divorce!

Why would these parents divorce one another, but not divorce their child? It is because they give unconditional love and forgiveness to the child, but not to one another. To live the Christian life and walk in freedom, we must give unconditional forgiveness.

Forgiveness releases an offender from expectation. Expectations can destroy a relationship! We are instructed to release offenders to God, the Righteous Judge, who will deal with all injustice.

Remember how King Saul pursued David. Though David had served him faithfully, Saul tried to kill David five times! How did David respond? He honored the king! He did not react in kind, rather, he chose not to touch God's anointed one. David found the courage to forgive each offense.

God blessed him for his good heart. David found special favor with Jonathan, King Saul's oldest son. David learned how to lead and how to fight. He learned how to recruit capable men. By doing good and releasing his offender through forgiveness, God blessed David and dealt with his enemies.

THE ANOINTING SETS US FREE

The anointing of the Holy Spirit in our lives can also break strongholds and bring emotional healing. Notice Acts 10:38: "God anointed Jesus of Nazareth with the Holy Spirit and with power, who went about doing good and healing all who were oppressed by the devil, for God was with Him" (NIV).

Isaiah 10:27 explains that the yoke will be destroyed because of the anointing. It is not uncommon for habits, controlling influences (spiritual yokes) to be broken as we grow in the power of the Spirit. The power of God is stronger than a strong man. As the influence of the Holy Spirit pervades every corner of our being, the strong man of sinful desires is pushed out.

After identifying a stronghold in our life, we must attack it with the truth of God's Word and in the power and anointing of the Holy Spirit. By the laying on of hands (Acts 19:11–12), we receive the benefit of impartation. The faith and favor of the person ministering to us is transferred. Gifts of the Holy Spirit under the anointing of God's servant have great benefit.

Let me encourage you to seek the prayer of others, even as you pray for your own healing. Desperation, not exasperation, will bring us to an opportunity for change. When our pain is unbearable, we will call out for help.

The church is a place of refuge for the hurting. "Is anyone among you sick? Let him call for the elders of the church, and let them pray over him, anointing him with oil in the name of the Lord. And the prayer of faith will save the sick, and the Lord will raise him up. And if he has committed sins, he will be forgiven. Confess your trespasses to one another, and pray for one another, that you may be healed. The effective, fervent prayer of a righteous man avails much" (James 5:14–16, NKJV).

Confession is a major part of the victory over wounded emotions. It makes us accountable to another believer. Hidden things cannot hide in the light!

It is very difficult to be transparent and honest, but if we are going to experience change, we must admit who we are and what has happened to us. Believers who have been forgiven and set free from emotional pain are most likely to be our greatest supporters. Having experienced pain and healing, they sympathize! They understand! Through the ministry of a church fellowship, we will discover acceptance and grace—important elements in a healing environment.

Alcoholics Anonymous has learned the power of accountability. Members confess their faults honestly to the group. One might say, "Hello, my name is Larry, and I am an alcoholic." We must also share the truth about ourselves.

Allow me to introduce you to people in the Bible who were touched by God's power and grace.

- "Hello, I am Hosea's wife, and I was a prostitute."

- "My name is Jacob, and I was a liar."

- "I am Paul, and I took part in killing and jailing Christians."

- "Hi, I am Peter, and I had a problem with anger."

Confession opens us to the covering of the church. It brings us to a place where the anointing and power of God's Word, and the support and acceptance of others, can be released into our life.

Recently in a Sunday night service, the atmosphere of worship and praise impacted two young ladies present. It was a time of unusual intimacy with God. Unsolicited, one young lady stood and tearfully told of being molested when she was a young teenager. When she had completed her remarks, the other young lady stood and told her story. Can you imagine the risk they took to share these harsh realities? As they opened themselves honestly before the congregation, the room filled with compassion. Words cannot describe what the moment did for those young ladies and for the church. Because the women felt comfortable and loved enough to trust others with their deepest hurts, they affirmed the ministry of the congregation.

CALL OUT TO THE LORD

The Bible is filled with the benefits of deliverance that come by calling out to the Lord.

> "In my distress I cried to the Lord, and He heard me. Deliver my soul, O Lord, from lying lips and from a deceitful tongue" (Psalms 120:1–2, NKJV).

> "The righteous cry out, and the Lord hears, and delivers them out of all their troubles" (Psalms 34:17, NKJV).

> "They cried out to the Lord in their trouble, and He saved them out of their distresses. He sent His word and healed them, and delivered them from their destructions" (Psalms 107:19–20, NKJV).

As believers, we have the great blessing of using the name of Jesus. When addressing the enemy of our soul, we must not come against him in our flesh or weakness. We overcome him by the word of our testimony and the blood of the Lamb (Revelation 12:11). When we speak the name of Jesus under His authority, the enemy must leave!

"At the name of Jesus every knee should bow, in heaven and on earth and under the earth, and every tongue acknowledge that Jesus Christ is Lord, to the glory of God the Father" (Philippians 2:10–11, NIV).

Having repented of the actions that have opened the door to oppressive spirits, we are on solid ground to cast down imaginations and bring every thought into captivity to the obedience of Christ (2 Corinthians 10:5). Take authority in Jesus' name and rebuke every manifestation of that stronghold in your life! Refuse to give a place to the enemy.

Begin to yield your body as an instrument for righteousness. Ignore the enticing voice of that oppressive spirit that wants you to revert to previous behavior and feelings.

As you exercise your will in obedience to God's Word, your spiritual person will grow stronger, and the enemy's grip will grow weaker. You will gain ground steadily, until you come into the full freedom God desires for His children.

CHAPTER SEVEN
DISCUSSION QUESTIONS

1. Is it possible to control our thoughts? If so, how? (pg. 66)

2. How can we forgive our offenders? (pg. 67)

3. How is it made possible for us to forgive ourselves?

4. Why does forgiveness bring healing?

5. Is forgiveness for a moment or an ongoing process? Discuss your answer. (pg. 68)

6. What harm does expectation bring into a relationship? (pg. 68)

7. How does confession bring healing? (pg. 70)

"I commend to you the ministry of Pastor Glenn Dorsey. As you read "Out of the Snare", you will gain spiritual insights and scriptural instructions to enhance your quest for victory. I read his book with much profit. Especially helpful is chapter 5, "What Must I Surrender to be Free?" His book contains answers that I will surely share with others and those I counsel."

–Mrs. Johanna (Alton) Garrison

"Desert nomads have a proverb: The greatest sin is to have water and be unwilling to share it. Glenn Dorsey has found water and is willing to share it. He has paid the price to drill to a deeper level of God's Word and locate life-changing answers. His answers are given from the perspective of long years of pastoral ministry, personal experience and a willingness to identify the presence of demonic influence in today's world."

–Jim Bennett, D. Miss.

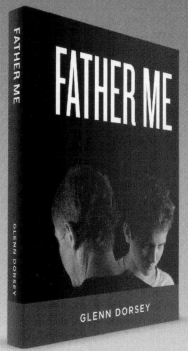

Made in the USA
Columbia, SC
19 January 2022